THE BATTLE OF FREDERICKSBURG

W. Scott Ingram

BLACKBIRCH PRESS

THOMSON
GALE

Detroit • New York • San Diego • San Francisco
Boston • New Haven, Conn. • Waterville, Maine
London • Munich

Published by Blackbirch Press
10911 Technology Place
San Diego, CA 92127

e-mail: customerservice@galegroup.com
Web site: http://www.galegroup.com/blackbirch

Printed in China

10 9 8 7 6 5 4 3 2 1

Photo credits:
Cover, pages 7, 14, 17, 18, 20, 22 (top) © North Wind Picture Archives; pages 8, 21 (bottom) © The Library of Congress; pages 10, 11, 13, 26, 29 © National Archives; pages 21 (top and center), 22 (bottom) © Dover Publications; page 28 © Corbis.

Library of Congress Cataloging-in-Publication Data
Ingram, Scott (William Scott)
The Battle of Fredericksburg / by W. Scott Ingram.
p. cm. — (The Civil War)
Includes index.
Summary: Details the Civil War battle of Fredericksburg, Virginia, and profiles some of the key figures involved in what was a decisive victory for the Confederacy.
ISBN 1-56711-560-8 (hardcover: alk. paper)
1. Fredericksburg (Va.), Battle of, 1862—Juvenile Literature. [1. Fredericksburg (Va.), Battle of, 1862. 2. United States—History—Civil War, 1861-1865—Campaigns.] I. Title. II. Civil War (Blackbirch Press).

E474.85 .I54 2002 2001004352
973. 7'33—dc21

CONTENTS

PREFACE: THE CIVIL WAR

Nearly 150 years after the final shots were fired, the Civil War remains one of the key events in U. S. history. The enormous loss of life alone makes it tragically unique: More Americans died in Civil War battles than in all other American wars combined. More Americans fell at the Battle of Gettysburg than during any battle in American military history. And, in one day at the Battle of Antietam, more Americans were killed and wounded than in any other day in American military history.

As tragic as the loss of life was, however, it is the principles over which the war was fought that make it uniquely American. Those beliefs—equality and freedom—are the foundation of American democracy, our basic rights. It was the bitter disagreement about the exact nature of those rights that drove our nation to its bloodiest war.

The disagreements grew in part from the differing economies of the North and South. The warm climate and wide-open areas of the Southern states were ideal for an economy based on agriculture. In the first half of the 19th century, the main cash crop was cotton, grown on large farms called plantations. Slaves, who were brought to the United States from Africa, were forced to do the backbreaking work of planting and harvesting cotton. They also provided the other labor necessary to keep plantations running. Slaves were bought and sold like property, and had been critical to the Southern economy since the first Africans came to America in 1619.

The suffering of African Americans under slavery is one of the great tragedies in American history. And the debate over whether the United States government had the right to forbid slavery—in both Southern states and in new territories—was a dispute that overshadowed the first 80 years of our history.

For many Northerners, the question of slavery was one of morality and not economics. Because the Northern economy was based on manufacturing rather than agriculture, there was little need for slave labor. The primary economic need of Northern states was a protective tax known as a tariff that would make imported goods more expensive than goods made in the North. Tariffs forced Southerners to buy Northern goods and made them economically dependent on the North, a fact that led to deep resentment among Southerners.

Economic control did not matter to the anti-slavery Northerners known as abolitionists. Their conflict with the South was over slavery. The idea that the federal government could outlaw slavery was perfectly reasonable. After all, abolitionists contended, our nation was founded on the idea that all people are created equal. How could slavery exist in such a country?

For the Southern states that joined the Confederacy, the freedom from unfair taxation and the right to make their own decisions about slavery was as important a principle as equality. For most Southerners, the right of states to decide what is best for its citizens was the most important principle guaranteed in the Constitution.

The conflict over these principles generated sparks throughout the decades leading up to the Civil War. The importance of keeping an equal number of slave and free states in the Union became critical to Southern lawmakers in Congress in those years. In 1820, when Maine and Missouri sought admission to the Union, the question was settled by the Missouri Compromise: Maine was admitted as a free state, Missouri as a slave state, thus maintaining a balance in Congress. The compromise stated that all future territories north of the southern boundary of Missouri would enter the Union as free states, those south of it would be slave states.

In 1854, however, the Kansas-Nebraska Act set the stage for the Civil War. That act repealed the Missouri Compromise and, by declaring that the question of slavery should be decided by residents of the territory, set off a rush of pro- and anti-slavery settlers to the new land. Violence between the two sides began almost immediately and soon "Bleeding Kansas" became a tragic chapter in our nation's story.

With Lincoln's election on an anti-slavery platform in 1860, the disagreement over the power of the federal government reached its breaking point. South Carolina became the first state to secede from the Union, followed by Mississippi, Florida, Alabama, Georgia, Louisiana, Virginia, Texas, North Carolina, Tennessee, and Arkansas. Those eleven states became the Confederate States of America. Confederate troops fired the first shots of the Civil War at Fort Sumter, South Carolina, on April 12, 1861. Those shots began a four-year war in which thousands of Americans—Northerners and Southerners—would give, in President Lincoln's words, "the last full measure of devotion."

INTRODUCTION: "LIE DOWN— YOU'LL ALL BE KILLED!"

By early afternoon on December 13, 1862, the sun had burned away the morning mist over Fredericksburg, Virginia. The city sat on the banks of the Rappahannock River, halfway between Washington, D.C. and the Confederate capital of Richmond. West of Fredericksburg, in an area known as Marye's Heights, the crack of rifles and the roar of cannons drowned out the cries of dying men.

Several waves of Union troops had tried—and failed—to drive out Rebel troops dug in behind a stone wall at the base of the heights. Now, as a third assault force gathered, Federals looked across an open field dotted with dead, dying, and wounded comrades. A Rebel officer observed that this was not war, it was "murder." Yet Union commanders continued to send their men to almost certain death.

The order to attack was given, and the blue lines moved forward. Immediately, Rebel riflemen, standing two rows deep behind the wall, sprang into action. One row fired and stepped back to reload. The second row stepped forward, fired, then stepped back. On either side of the constant fire, Rebel artillery added a murderous steel crossfire of shells, canister shot, railroad iron, and plow blades.

The Confederates cut the Union troops to shreds. Federals climbed over and around bodies piled three deep. Many lost their footing on blood-slick grass. Some who fell were not hit—they simply refused to get up. They grabbed at others who passed, trying to pull them down and save them. "Lie down! You'll all be killed," came the cry.

Incredibly, there were seven failed Union assaults that day. By nightfall, more than 7,000 Federals lay dead and dying, their blood freezing on the icy ground.

Confederate troops fired from behind stone walls during the Battle of Fredericksburg.

GATHERING AT THE RAPPAHANNOCK

★ ★ ★ ★ ★

By the autumn of 1862, the Civil War had gone on for more than a year. What both sides had hoped would be a brief conflict had become a brutal, bloody struggle. The Confederates' well-trained, fast-moving Rebels had defeated the vastly larger and better-equipped Union forces time and again.

In September 1862, Rebels under General Robert E. Lee attempted their first invasion of the North. When Confederate and Union forces met at Antietam Creek near Sharpsburg, Maryland, the ensuing battle became the bloodiest single day in U.S. history, with a total of more than 23,000 dead and wounded.

Lincoln hoped for a Union victory before the end of 1862.

Antietam was considered a Union victory because the Confederate advance was halted, even though Union forces gained barely a mile of ground. Though costly, the victory did produce one important result: It encouraged President Abraham Lincoln to issue his Emancipation Proclamation, which freed all slaves in Confederate territory as of January 1, 1863.

Most Union supporters, however, hoped for a more resounding Union victory before the turn of the year to give added weight to the proclamation. Lincoln himself wanted the enormous Union forces to pursue Lee back into Virginia. At 115,000 men, the Army of the Potomac was the Union's largest fighting force, and outnumbered Lee's Army of Northern Virginia by nearly 40,000 soldiers.

Burnside Replaces McClellan

As September drew to a close, Lee and his two closest advisors, Generals Thomas "Stonewall" Jackson and James Longstreet, expected the Union army under General George McClellan to be in fierce pursuit. In fact, the president urged McClellan to "press closely" to Lee.

McClellan, however, a West Point graduate and career military man, paid scant attention to Lincoln's orders because the president lacked military experience. Frustrated, Lincoln finally relieved the popular general of his command on November 7, 1862, and appointed McClellan's close friend, General Ambrose E. Burnside, commander of the Army of the Potomac. Lincoln had actually offered Burnside the position twice before, but Burnside told the president that he did not feel qualified to command an army.

His colleagues agreed. General George Meade, who would later command forces at Gettysburg, wrote that Burnside "had some positive qualifications, but he . . . was deficient in that enlarged mental capacity which is essential in a commander."

Even junior officers doubted Burnside. A captain from Massachusetts wrote of him, "Never has a man risen to such great heights on so slim a foundation."

In early November, Burnside named three officers to command the three divisions of the Army of the Potomac: William B. Franklin, Edwin Sumner, and Joseph Hooker. Opposing Burnside was a Confederate army of 78,000 men spread thinly across northern Virginia.

Half of Lee's force was under James Longstreet in the town of Culpeper, Virginia. This force defended Richmond against a direct Union attack. The other half of Lee's force, under Stonewall Jackson, was stationed west, across the Blue Ridge Mountains in the Shenandoah Valley. This fast-moving force was assigned to harass Burnside's vulnerable lines of supply.

Lincoln assumed that Burnside's strategy would be to use his larger force to defeat Longstreet and force Jackson to give up his position. Burnside, however, realized that if he attacked Longstreet, the Confederates would retreat to a tighter defensive line closer to Richmond. Burnside also knew that his force would become more vulnerable because his supply lines would be extended. The other problem was that advancing in Longstreet's direction left Washington,

D.C. open to a Confederate counterattack, a specialty of the Rebels fighting under Jackson.

Because of these concerns, Burnside decided to take a direct southern route toward Richmond through Fredericksburg, Virginia. That route followed Union-controlled rivers, thus making supply lines easier to maintain. It also kept Union troops between the Rebels and Washington.

The main problem with the Fredericksburg route was the Rappahannock River. At Culpeper, 30 miles west of the city, the Rappahannock is little more than a stream that can be crossed easily. By the time it reaches Fredericksburg, however, it broadens to a 400-foot-wide river that must be crossed by bridge. Rebels had destroyed the original bridges early in the war. Union troops intended to overcome this challenge with pontoons—portable bridges that floated on boats.

Lincoln was disappointed by Burnside's strategy. Nevertheless, he approved his new commander's plan, advising Burnside that the plan "will succeed if you move rapidly; otherwise not."

Responding to the president's advice, Burnside ordered 65-year-old General Edwin Sumner and his division to break camp on November 15. Two days later, Sumner's huge force reached Falmouth, a few miles upriver from Fredericksburg. Across the Rappahannock, about 1,000 Confederates defended Fredericksburg.

Sumner attacked immediately. While Northern howitzers fired shells into the town to harass the defenders, Sumner ordered a New York

The Rappahannock River at Fredericksburg is 400 feet wide.

Pontoon bridges allowed Union forces to cross the Rappahannock.

brigade that consisted largely of Irish immigrants to cross the river, which was shoulder deep at Falmouth, and take control of Fredericksburg.

The Irish Brigade was halfway across the river when Burnside rode up. Concerned that the autumn rains might cause the Rappahannock to rise quickly and separate the brigade from the main force, Burnside ordered Sumner to recall his troops.

Days Become Weeks

Burnside's plan to send his whole force across the river at one time stalled when the pontoon boats were delayed. On November 24, after more than a week of struggling along muddy roads and crossing flooded creeks, the engineers finally delivered the bridges.

Unfortunately for Burnside's army, Longstreet's corps had reached Fredericksburg five days earlier. By November 22, two days before the pontoons arrived, the Confederates had established a strong seven-mile-long defensive position on the hills behind Fredericksburg, outside the range of Union artillery.

Lee had originally ordered Longstreet's troops to the North Anna River, the best defensive position between Fredericksburg and

Richmond. To allow his army time to reach the North Anna, he sent two divisions toward Fredericksburg to obstruct the Union army's advance.

When the Confederate divisions reached Fredericksburg, however, they discovered that the Federals had not crossed the river. Hearing this, Lee immediately redirected General Longstreet's entire force to Fredericksburg.

On November 21, Stonewall Jackson had ordered his corps east to join Longstreet. It was a cold, brutal march over rocky ground. Few Confederates had shoes. Even under such conditions, however, Jackson's men reached Fredericksburg on December 3. They had marched 175 miles in just 12 days. Jackson established his forces south of town, covering the Rappahannock River between Hamilton's Crossing and Port Royal.

Burnside now knew he would need a good plan to succeed in crossing the river. In truth, he had few options. Upriver from Fredericksburg stood Banks' Ford, a possible crossing. But Longstreet's troops were positioned nearby, and the river's steep banks made climbing slippery and dangerous.

Another Union option was crossing downriver between Fredericksburg and Port Royal. Union scouts reported only a small force of Confederates in that area. Still hoping to get between Southern forces and Richmond, Burnside decided to cross the river at Skinker's Neck. No sooner had Union engineers begun to improve the river roads there, however, than Jackson's corps arrived and established a position.

Rebels Dig In

While Union forces scouted the Rappahannock, Rebel forces under Longstreet—considered the greatest defensive strategist of the war—built earthworks on the riverbank and on the hills southwest of Fredericksburg. They also dug emplacements for Longstreet's formidable artillery units. The big guns were perched on Marye's (pronounced Marie's) Heights and positioned at angles to create a deadly crossfire.

When Longstreet, a perfectionist, requested that his artillery commander add still another piece to the already crowded emplacements, the man replied: "General, a chicken could not live on that field when we open fire on it."

For the men on both sides of the Rappahannock, the weeks before the battle were uncomfortable, boring, and lonely. Soldiers' hands, feet, and beards froze during the cold nights. As was true throughout the war, Rebel soldiers suffered more than their Union opponents did. Most lacked warm clothing and shoes. There were no tents. Shelters were made from rubber tarps or blankets strung on tree limbs or brush covered with leaves.

The cold weather passed, however, and daytime temperatures rose into the 50s. Troops on either side of the river began friendly, teasing conversations with their counterparts on the other side. Some Rebels built toy sailboats and used them to send small packages of tobacco across the river. Union guards took the tobacco and sent back coffee. On several occasions, soldiers from one army actually crossed the river under a flag of truce to talk and trade newspapers with enemy troops.

On December 5, several inches of snow fell. Burnside knew that with winter approaching, he could wait no longer: His army would have to cross at Fredericksburg itself.

Across the River

By early December, Burnside concluded that attacking the center of

Union artillery is positioned across the Rappahannock from Fredericksburg.

the Confederate line, on the heights behind Fredericksburg, could divide Rebel forces that he believed were thinly stretched. Burnside assembled his division commanders on December 9 to present this strategy.

Immediately, Generals William Franklin and Joseph Hooker opposed the idea, while Edwin Sumner supported his commander. Sumner's staff, however, strongly opposed Burnside's plan.

When Burnside was told of the objections to the plan, he called his junior officers to Sumner's headquarters. "I have heard your criticisms, gentlemen, and your complaints," Burnside is reported to have said. "You know how reluctantly I assumed the responsibility of command. Your duty is not to throw cold water, but to aid me loyally with your advice and hearty service."

Fighting on the streets in Fredericksburg was fierce.

Burnside ordered the construction of three pontoon bridges to begin at 3 A.M. on December 11. He expected to have his entire force across the Rappahannock River by nightfall.

As the troops left camp and reassembled closer to the river, gloom settled over the men. Staring at the light of campfires on the heights, one Union officer wrote a farewell to his son: "I expect to be sacrificed tomorrow. Goodbye old Boy & if tomorrow night finds me dead remember me kindly."

As 3 A.M. approached, army engineers worked the boats off the wagons and dragged them to the water. The first boats in the water were anchored to the shore. Other boats were connected to the anchor boats by timbers and planks, forming the walkway of the bridge. Slowly the bridges stretched across the dark, rushing water.

On the Rebel side, the troops in the city were commanded by General William Barksdale, a former congressman from Mississippi and an outspoken supporter of Southern secession before the war.

Darkness and dense fog prevented Barksdale's men from seeing exactly what was happening.

At first light, Southern cannons fired two quick shots, giving the signal that the Union army was on the move. Union engineers heard the signal, yet the bridges were still 100 feet from the opposite shore as the sun rose. The moment they could make out the shapes of Union soldiers, the Confederates opened fire. "The bullets of the enemy rained upon my bridge," a Union commander wrote. "They went whizzing and spitting by and around me, patting on the splashing water and thugging through the boats."

Wounded Union soldiers retreated, crawling along the pontoons until they could be pulled to safety on the muddy riverbank. In response to the Confederate fire, more than 50 Union cannons fired into Fredericksburg. Union engineers took advantage of the covering fire to resume work on the bridges. At each attempt, however, sharpshooters drove them back to the shore.

Burnside had not anticipated such strong resistance, and he had no clear plan to beat back the Rebels and allow his men to cross. Finally, he turned to his artillery. For the next eight hours, nearly 150 cannons shelled the empty town. "Tons of iron were hurled against the place," wrote one Rebel. "The deafening roar of cannon and bursting shells, falling walls and chimneys, brick and timbers flying through the air, houses set on fire, the smoke adding to the already heavy fog, the bursting of flames through the housetops, made a scene which has no parallel in history."

Shells and falling masonry killed many Southern troops, but the survivors continued to fire at the bridges. By afternoon, the Union army was no closer to crossing the river than it had been at dawn.

General Henry Hunt, commander of the Union artillery, suggested sending soldiers across the Rappahannock in the pontoon boats to push Confederates from the water's edge. The plan was extremely risky, but Burnside had no other choice—the Union had already been delayed nearly 12 hours.

Shortly after 3 P.M., Hunt's guns began a heavy bombardment, while volunteers from the 7th Michigan prepared to launch the boats. Suddenly the big guns were silent, and the Federals scrambled into

★
Union forces used hot air balloons to observe Confederate troop positions before the battle.
★

the 30-foot-long boats. Rowing and poling with all their might, about 70 men went across in the first assault. Bullets zipped into the water around them and splintered the planks of the boats.

On the Rebel side of the river, the Michigan volunteers jumped out of the boats and assembled a battle line. Charging up into town, they entered the houses along the river. Within minutes, the Federal troops had established a position to protect the next group across. As fighting continued in bloody house-to-house skirmishes, boats traveled back and forth across the river bringing additional troops, and Union soldiers cheered as each boatload reached the Confederate side. "This flash of bravery had done what scores of batteries and tons of metal had failed to accomplish," wrote a Massachusetts soldier.

Fredericksburg, however, was still not under Union control. Confederate squads, hidden in cellars or attics, shot Union troops who had no idea where their enemy was hidden. A Massachusetts company lost 10 of 30 men in five minutes. Another unit of 300 lost 97 men while advancing only 50 yards.

As the early dusk settled on the town, the pontoon bridges were finally completed. Regiments began to charge across the river. By nightfall, Union troops controlled most of the streets in Fredericksburg, but the Confederate troops had killed and wounded hundreds of men and delayed the crossing.

A City Destroyed

It took the remainder of the 115,000-man Union army most of the following day, December 12, to cross the river into Fredericksburg. The Federals entered a deserted city. Frightened civilians had abandoned their homes over the previous weeks as armies had gathered. Arriving Union troops wandered through the empty streets of Fredericksburg—a historic town of classic Southern colonial homes filled with expensive furnishings, artwork, and other valuable items.

Many troops were bored from weeks of inactivity. Others were on edge from the brutal fighting the day before. Those emotions surfaced

This engraving shows Fredericksburg after Union troops ransacked the city late in 1862.

in a violent outburst. Federal soldiers rampaged through town, and stole whatever they could carry from the banks and the library. Homes and businesses were torn apart and ravaged. Men burned books, paintings, pianos, and furniture in huge bonfires. The destruction of Fredericksburg was one of the worst acts of vandalism during the Civil War.

Strategic Uncertainties

While Union troops destroyed Fredericksburg, Burnside and his commanding officers met in a house back across the Rappahannock to plan battle strategy. Burnside decided to attack the Confederates at two points along their line. The main attack would be launched south of town against Stonewall Jackson's corps. Under Burnside's plan, William Franklin's Left Grand Division, with the support of half of Hooker's Center Grand Division—a force of 60,000 men—would assault Jackson's right flank at Prospect Hill. Once the Southerners were in retreat, Edwin Sumner's Right Grand Division, reinforced by the other half of Hooker's division, would advance from town and strike Longstreet's positions at Marye's Heights.

Late on the 12th, Burnside met with Franklin and Franklin's corps commanders. Franklin, certain that all present understood the planned strategy, was ready to send his generals back to their troops to have them assemble for an attack at first light on the 13th. All he needed was the official order from Burnside to do so.

Burnside, however, failed to issue the order. Instead, he simply left the meeting and returned to his own headquarters. The evening passed while Franklin and his commanders waited for a final order from Burnside.

Attack on Jackson

Shortly before dawn, Burnside's orders finally arrived by courier. Strangely, Burnside had decided overnight to have Franklin hold back most of his force. The Union was ordered to attack the Rebels with only a division—about 5,000 men.

Union artillery fired shells into Fredericksburg from across the Rappahannock.

Not only were Burnside's orders a puzzle, their arrival just before sunrise meant that the morning mist—good cover for attackers—would burn off by the time the Federals were even assembled to attack. Franklin sent orders down the line for General John Reynolds to move his First Corps into position. Reynolds's Corps consisted of three fighting units. One, commanded by General Abner Doubleday, was on the far left of the attack line. George Meade's Pennsylvania unit was in the center. General John Gibbons's division was positioned on the right.

The Federal attack lines came into view about 1,000 yards from the Rebels of A.P. Hill's division. Neither Hill nor his commander, Stonewall Jackson, realized that they had left a break 600 yards wide in their defensive position. At 10:00 A.M., the Federal force advanced. As Meade's and Gibbons's Federals moved out, Union artillery opened fire, clearing the way for the advancing troops.

Behind Rebel lines, a young artillery officer, Major John Pelham, had an idea for disrupting the attackers. Pelham asked his commander, General Jeb Stuart, if he could take two big guns down a side road to Hamilton's Crossing and attack the Federal lines from the side in a flanking action. Stuart agreed, but emphasized that Pelham had to return to Rebel lines when ordered. Once in position with two cannons, Pelham fired canister shot into the Federal lines, which drove one brigade to the muddy ground for cover. Immediately, Federal artillery returned fire. One of Pelham's two guns was destroyed, but the courageous officer continued to fire his remaining cannon until ammunition ran out. Pelham's one-gun assault halted the Union advance for almost an hour.

At about 11:00 A.M., Meade ordered his troops to continue their advance. About 800 yards from the Rebels, Confederate guns opened fire and Meade's men again hit the mud. A fierce artillery duel then broke out between Union and Confederate gunners, with Union artillery units getting the best of the fight. The battle killed so many horses that the veterans referred to the Southern position as "Dead Horse Hill" for years afterward.

An Inequality Among Commanders

Most historians agree that the overwhelming Confederate victory at Fredericksburg was due more to the difference in the leadership qualities of the commanders than to fighting abilities of the troops. The three main Confederate commanders—Lee, Longstreet, and Jackson—were considered masters of tactical warfare and are well known. On the other hand, the main Union commanders—Burnside, Franklin, Hooker, and Sumner—were considered competent, but nothing more.

Ambrose Burnside

Ambrose Burnside had turned down the position of commander of the Army of the Potomac twice before Fredericksburg. Like that of his predecessor and friend, George McClellan, Burnside's overcautious style ultimately proved his undoing. Had he allowed the initial Union force that reached the banks of the Rappahannock to cross in late November, the town would have fallen. Had he also committed more troops to the initial stages of the battle against Jackson, the result might have been more favorable. Burnside, who had little respect from subordinates, was replaced shortly after the Fredericksburg campaign. Today, he is remembered chiefly for the style of his facial hair, a style that became known as "sideburns."

William Franklin finished first in the Class of 1843 at West Point, but the Civil War ended his military career. His inability to get clear directions from Burnside meant that his troops went into battle against Jackson without proper support. Burnside blamed Franklin for the loss, and Franklin, in turn, sent a letter to Lincoln declaring Burnside an incompetent leader. Both men left the military by 1865.

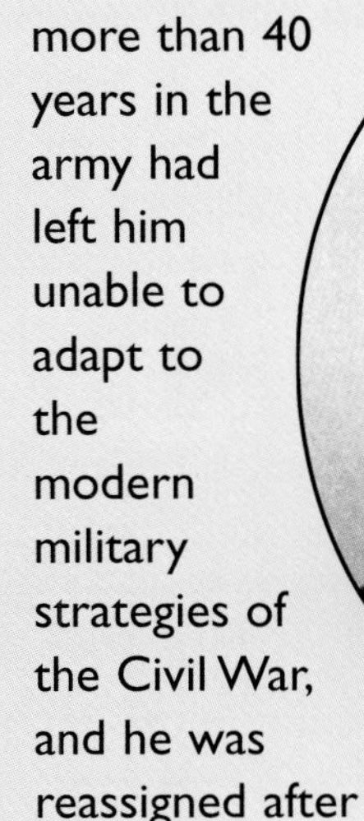

William Franklin

Joseph Hooker was the general who finally decided to end the futile assaults at Marye's Heights. He replaced Burnside early in 1863 and lost at the Battle of Chancellorsville. "Fighting Joe" was well liked by troops, but his habit of openly criticizing his superior officers made him very unpopular.

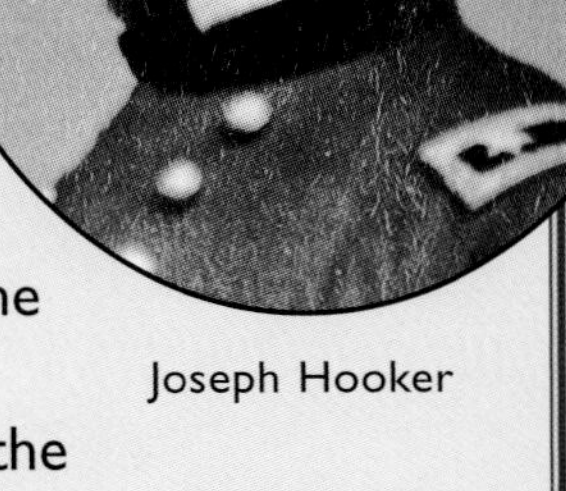

Joseph Hooker

Edwin Sumner, known among the troops as "Bull," was, at age 65, the oldest Union commander on the battlefield. His more than 40 years in the army had left him unable to adapt to the modern military strategies of the Civil War, and he was reassigned after the battle.

Edwin Sumner

George Meade

Eventually, Meade realized that if his troops did not move, they would be destroyed. As he prepared to advance, a Union shell hit a Confederate ammunition wagon, setting off a huge explosion. Meade saw his chance amid the smoky confusion. He ordered his men to charge. Suddenly, the Federals burst into the gap that Hill and Jackson had failed to notice.

The Federal line of attack pivoted quickly and surprised a Rebel brigade already under frontal attack and unprepared for a flank attack. The Rebels fell back from this double onslaught.

This event might have led to a Union victory. The blunders that followed, however, demonstrated the command problems that plagued the Union army early in the war and prevented it from capitalizing on its advantage.

Meade needed reinforcements for his battle-weary and depleted 1st Corps. He sent an aide back to General David Birney asking him to send in the fresh troops of the 6th Corps under his command. Birney, however, refused to obey a request from an officer of equal rank, stating that he would take orders only from Meade's commander, Reynolds.

Furious, Meade sent another officer back to Birney—and again Birney refused. Finally Meade, in a rage, rode back and cornered Birney, telling his colleague that he would take all responsibility for bypassing Reynolds on the chain of command. Birney agreed to that condition. By that time, however, Rebels under General Jubal Early had counterattacked. Meade's men, disorganized, exhausted, and taking heavy casualties, were pushed back, and the Federal line broke.

Rebel artillery moved forward and poured heavy fire into Federal ranks to keep them from re-forming. And casualties forced General Reynolds to serve on a cannon crew to protect retreating troops instead of coordinating efforts that might win the battle.

David Birney

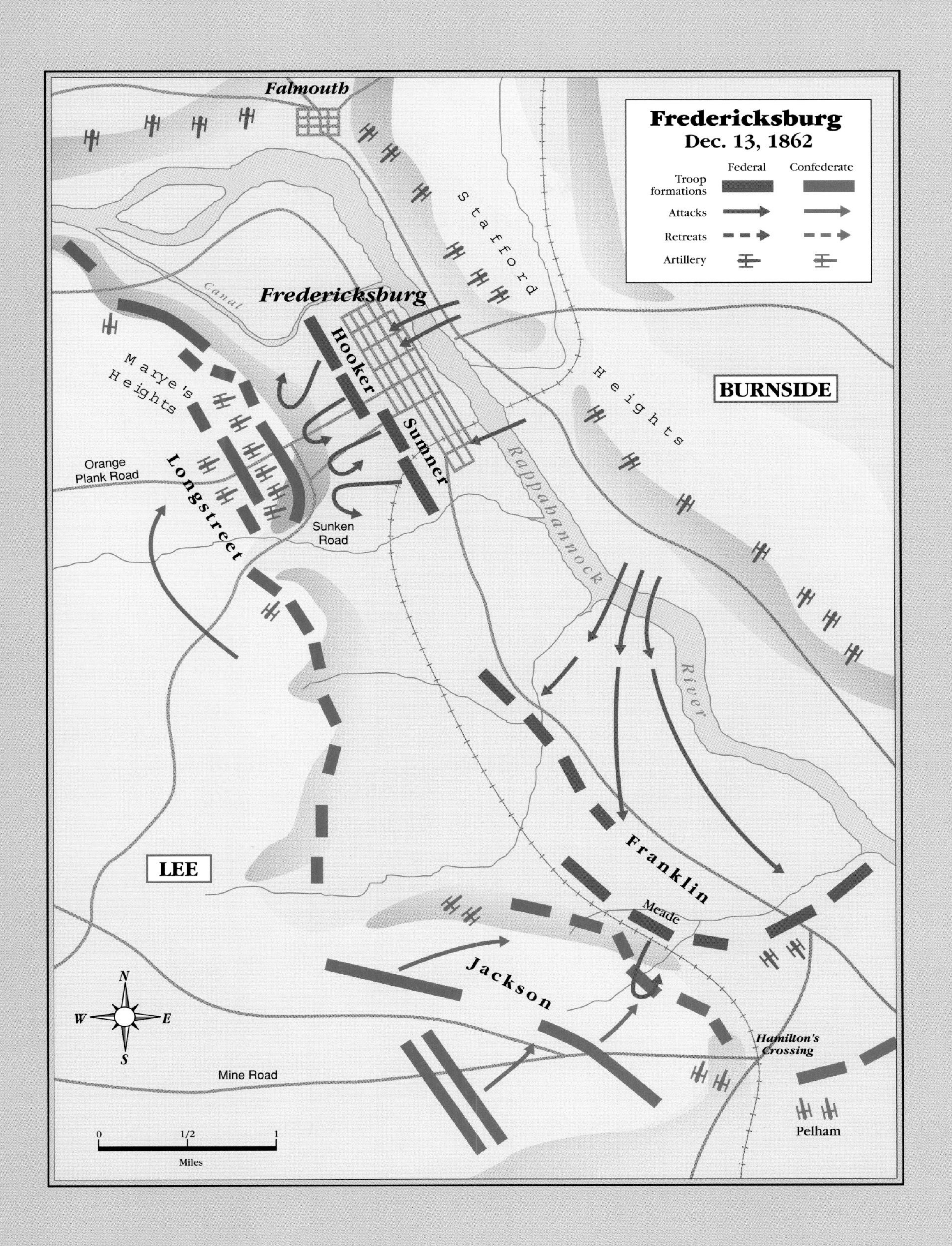

Fredericksburg
Dec. 13, 1862
Federal
Confederate
Troop formations
Attacks
Retreats
Artillery
Falmouth
Stafford
Heights
Fredericksburg
Canal
Marye's Heights
Hooker
Sumner
Longstreet
Orange Plank Road
Sunken Road
Rappahannock
River
BURNSIDE
LEE
Franklin
Meade
Jackson
Hamilton's Crossing
Mine Road
Pelham
N
S
E
W
0
1/2
1
Miles

The initial part of the battle for Fredericksburg could have ended in victory for either side. Union forces lost over 4,800 men. Jackson lost 3,400 men. The rest of the battle would not be so even.

Attack on Longstreet

While the fighting at the southern end of battleground was reaching its full fury, another battle was about to begin five miles to the north at the center of the Confederate line. There, into the heart of the Confederate defense, Burnside ordered a series of assaults. To attack the Rebels, the Federals would have to cross an open plain toward the high ground, a difficult task in any battle.

Despite the fact that the Federals had more than 60,000 men, the huge force was squeezed into a relatively small space that limited attacks to waves of approximately 5,000 men. These troops had to cross more than 600 yards of open ground to reach a Confederate force of nearly 7,000 soldiers on high ground behind secure fortifications.

On the morning of the 13th, while Franklin, Meade, and Doubleday initiated the fight against Jackson, Sumner's division and the remainder of Hooker's division assembled on the outskirts of Fredericksburg. Sumner ordered General Darius Couch to ready his Federal 2nd Corps for the first assault.

Union troops now faced the almost impossible task of overrunning the well-fortified Confederates. During their weeks of waiting for a Union attack, Southern soldiers had banked dirt against a wall to stop Union bullets and shells from penetrating the defense.

At noon, Sumner ordered the attack to commence. Couch's Union soldiers soon encountered a canal about 200 yards out, not shown on their maps, that ran across the plain. The Federals were forced to file in columns across three partially destroyed bridges that crossed the canal, which slowed the attack.

As soon as the first wave reassembled, the Rebels opened fire. Arranged in two lines behind the stone wall, the first row of Confederate riflemen fired, then stepped back to reload as the second line came forward and aimed. This rapid-fire technique was joined by artillery crossfire from the heights. Union soldiers were cut down like blades of grass. Within minutes the field was dotted with the killed and wounded. Survivors of the slaughter took cover behind dead comrades while they searched for a way to escape.

Like targets in a shooting gallery, the second wave of the Union attack marched in precise order behind the first wave. Rebel fire cut down nearly half of this group. Behind them followed the third wave, which got no closer than their fallen comrades before them. Within an hour, bodies lay three deep below the Rebel defenses at Marye's Heights. A whole division of men had nearly been wiped out. No Union soldiers had come within 150 yards of the wall.

At this point, a Union division under General Winfield S. Hancock lined up to continue the assault. Hancock rode among the three brigades in his division, shouting orders and urging his men to fight bravely. First to attack was a brigade under Colonel Samuel Zook, followed by the Irish Brigade under General Thomas Meagher, and finally by a brigade commanded by General John Caldwell. Zook's brigade was decimated. Survivors who tried to retreat tripped and fell over the growing piles of dead and wounded. Hancock later wrote that his men "melted like snow coming down on warm ground."

The last of Hancock's brigades followed Meagher's failed attack against the Rebel stronghold. This brigade also fell in the hail of bullets and shells. Hancock's division suffered nearly 2,100 dead, wounded, and missing—42 percent of his division, the largest percentage of loss to any division in any battle during the entire war.

Finally, Sumner ordered General Oliver Howard to send his brigades up over the same ground. Many soldiers in that wave later reported that the attack was slowed because they had to step over and around the dead, wounded, and those too frightened to move. The assault was made even more difficult by poor footing in the grass, which had become slippery with blood.

Howard's men soon met the same fate as the other Union troops that had charged the stone wall. As quickly as they reached the field, his troops were killed or pinned down.

As wave after wave of doomed Federals continued the futile attack, the Confederate High Command became concerned about its troop

★

Union troops had to cross more than 600 yards of wide open space to attack Longstreet's forces.

Union troops prepare to march into battle.

strength along the stone wall. Lee questioned whether Rebel defenses all along Marye's Heights could withstand wave after wave of Federals. Longstreet, who had been closer to the action, was certain that his defensive stand was solid. He told Lee that as long as his ammunition held out, his riflemen and artillery could kill all the Federals sent against his position. To back up his claim, Longstreet ordered reinforcements to add support along the wall. There were soon enough men to form four lines behind the stone and dirt barricade, doubling the murderous firepower.

As the slaughter continued, even the battle-hardened Rebels felt sickened. One Rebel later wrote, "We watched the fruitless charges, with their fearful slaughter until we were sick at heart. As I watched one line get swept away by one fearful blast from behind the wall, I forgot they were enemies and only remembered that they were men, and it is hard to see in cold blood, brave men die."

By 2 P.M., the Federals had sent four divisions up against the Rebel defenses. None had come within 50 yards of the target. Union commanders, realizing the futility of Burnside's plan, temporarily halted the charges.

"As Many Men as My Orders Require"

Around 2:30 P.M., Burnside gave orders from his headquarters for Franklin to renew his attack on Jackson in the south. Joseph Hooker was ordered to send his Grand Right Division against the forces at Marye's Heights. Franklin, believing that a renewed attack against Jackson was futile, simply ignored the order and refused to reassemble his troops.

Burnside's headquarters was more than five miles from the battlefield.

As Hooker's men prepared to attack, Hooker rode to the battlefield. There, he saw the incredible disaster that had struck the Federals. Quickly, he rode to Burnside's headquarters to report his observations and request that the order to attack be withdrawn.

Hooker left General Daniel Butterfield in charge. Butterfield felt he had to order his division into action to help relieve troops still trapped on the field by heavy fire. One by one the brigades were sent forward, only to suffer the same bloody fate. Hooker returned from his meeting with Burnside unable to convince his commander to stop the attacks. Looking across the field, Hooker decided to send General George Getty's unit into battle. Finally, as the sun sank lower, Hooker ordered all attacks stopped. His famously grim comment at that moment was that he had "lost as many men as my orders require."

By the evening of December 13, seven divisions had been ordered against the stone wall protecting Marye's Heights. The attacks resulted in more than 7,000 Union casualties and only 1,200 on the Confederate side. As night fell, Rebels broke out in wild yells of triumph. Observing his joyous men, who had destroyed the Union force, Lee remarked to Longstreet, "It is well that war is so terrible, else we should grow too fond of it."

The Long Night

As darkness descended, thousands of men lay dead and wounded on the field below Marye's Heights. Cries and moans echoed in the frigid air. Some soldiers bled to death, while others survived because the cold froze the blood in their wounds. Scavengers from both sides roamed the field stripping the dead of their shoes, clothes, weapons, and other possessions.

"Angel of Fredericksburg"

While his Rebel comrades celebrated their victory on the night of December 13, nineteen-year-old Confederate Sergeant Richard Kirkland of the 2nd South Carolina felt sick at heart. The pitiful sounds of wounded Union soldiers crying out for water was more than he could stand. Kirkland received reluctant approval from his commander to tend to the wounded. Slipping over the stone wall with as many wooden canteens as he could carry, he spent nearly two hours giving water to dying men, helping them to more comfortable positions, and leaving full canteens by their sides. Kirkland later fought at Gettysburg, and died in late 1863 at the Battle of Chickamauga. A statue honoring Kirkland, the "Angel of Marye's Heights," now stands at the Fredericksburg battlefield.

A statue honoring Richard Kirkland stands on Marye's Heights.

In the darkness, Rebel sharpshooters moved out from behind the wall to keep Union troops from moving. Union Lieutenant Colonel Joshua Chamberlain of the 20th Maine Regiment was among those trapped on the cold ground. Seriously wounded, he pulled the bodies of three dead men over him to provide warmth during the long night. When dawn broke, he regrouped with the other survivors for the retreat into Fredericksburg.

At noon on December 14, Burnside's commanders convinced him to pull his battered forces back across the Rappahannock. The rest of the day, the Federals worked to remove wounded men from the field and quickly bury as many of the dead as possible. So disfigured were many of the bodies from the slaughter that more than 85 percent of the graves at the Fredericksburg cemetery contain unknown soldiers.

Confederates awoke on December 15 to find the field abandoned. Of the 17,000 casualties, 13,000 had been Union troops. Although the battle of Fredericksburg was over, the tragic story of the campaign was not. Confederate commanders entered Fredericksburg to find it destroyed. Among Confederates, the feeling arose that the character of the war had turned, and it had become a battle of survival in which the enemy had to be crushed. Observing the ruin

When Confederate troops entered Fredericksburg after the battle, it was in ruins.

of Fredericksburg, Stonewall Jackson remarked, "We must do more than defeat their armies, we must destroy them."

Lincoln's hopes of winning political support for the Emancipation Proclamation with a military triumph had ended in disaster.

Postscript

By January 1863, the Army of the Potomac was still camped on the western side of the Rappahannock. As the winter settled in, Burnside decided to send his army in a flanking maneuver upriver against Fredericksburg. Unfortunately for the Union troops, this maneuver began during torrential rains that turned roads into vast oceans of neck-deep mud.

The infamous "mud march" failed to do anything except further lower respect for Burnside among Union troops and officers. In fact, Burnside became so enraged with the lack of respect that he sent a memo to Lincoln demanding that certain officers be removed or he would resign. In response, Lincoln replaced Burnside with Joseph Hooker, which officially ended the Fredericksburg campaign.

Bitter memories of that event, however, remained for both sides. After another Confederate victory at Chancellorsville in May 1863, Lee invaded the North once again. This time, he alerted officers to warn troops that anyone engaging in vandalism like that of the Union soldiers at Fredericksburg would be shot.

Lee's invasion ended at Gettysburg, Pennsylvania. The final day of the battle was marked by a charge of Confederate troops—today known as "Pickett's Charge"—that was in many ways as hopeless as the Union assault at Marye's Heights. As the shattered Confederate troops retreated from that charge, Union troops were heard to call after them, "Fredericksburg! Fredericksburg! Fredericksburg!"

Glossary

artillery mounted guns, such as cannons or missile launchers
barricade a barrier, especially one put up hastily for defense; the action of blocking with a barrier
brigade a military unit smaller than a division and composed of one or more units of infantry or armored forces and supporting units
corps a tactical subdivision of an army; or a specialized branch of an army
decimate to destroy or kill a large part of
division the smallest tactical unit of an army large enough to fight on its own for long periods of combat; larger than a regiment or brigade but smaller than a corps, having between 12,000 and 20,000 soldiers
emplacement a prepared position for weapons or military equipment
fortification something constructed for defense, like a trench or a fort
pontoon any of a row of boats or floating objects used to support a temporary bridge
regiment a small body of troops which is responsible for recruiting, equipping, and training new soldiers
sharpshooter a type of soldier especially accurate with a gun
vandalism intentional destruction of public or private property

For More Information

Books

Collier, Christopher. *The Civil War: 1860–1865* (Drama of American History). Tarrytown, NY: Benchmark Books, 2000.
Graves, Kerry A. *The Civil War* (America Goes to War). Mankato, MN: Bridgestone Books, 2001.
Sandler, Martin W. *Civil War* (Library of Congress Books). New York: Harpercollins, 2001.
Smolinski, Diane. *Battles of the Civil War* (Americans at War: The Civil War). Westport, CT: Heinemann Library, 2001.

Web Sites

Fredericksburg
Learn more about the battle of Fredericksburg and famous Civil War generals—**www.militaryhistoryonline.com/fredericksburg/**
Fredericksburg and Spotsylvania National Military Park
See photos of and learn more about the Fredericksburg battlefield—**www.nps.gov/frsp**

Index